PURE PLANET

A Look at Air and Water Quality

by Heather DiLorenzo Williams

NORWOOD HOUSE PRESS

Norwood House Press

For more information about Norwood House Press please visit our website at www.norwoodhousepress.com or call 866-565-2900.
© 2023 Norwood House Press.

Credits

Editor: Mari Bolte
Designer: Sara Radka

Photo Credits

page 1: ©Roberto Moiola / Sysaworld / Getty Images; page 3: ©steinphoto / Getty Images; page 3: ©Lowell Georgia / Getty Images; page 3: ©Gary Bell / Getty Images; page 5: ©Getty Images / Stringer / Getty Images; page 8: ©dacascas / Shutterstock; page 9: ©narvikk / Getty Images; page 10: ©Don and Melinda Crawford / Getty Images; page 12: ©Hidalgo Calatayud Espinoza/dpa/picture-alliance / Newscom; page 14: ©DC Productions / Getty Images; page 16: ©Livia Lazar / EyeEm / Getty Images; page 17: ©Martin Puddy / Getty Images; page 18: ©Keystone / Stringer / Getty Images; page 19: ©USEPA / flickr; page 20: ©Jupiterimages / Getty Images; page 22: ©sinology / Getty Images; page 23: ©petovarga / Getty Images; page 24: ©Brayden Bise / EyeEm / Getty Images; page 25: ©bravo1954 / Getty Images; page 27: ©Monty Rakusen / Getty Images; page 29: ©BanksPhotos / Getty Images; page 30: ©Leonardo Casas/Eyepix/Cover Images / Newscom; page 31: ©piranka / Getty Images; page 33: ©Ippei Naoi / Getty Images; page 34: ©Douglas Sacha / Getty Images; page 35: ©Catherine McQueen / Getty Images; page 36: ©Cover Images/ZUMAPRESS / Newscom; page 40: ©rmitsch / Getty Images; page 41: ©Jeff J Mitchell / Staff / Getty Images; page 42: ©SpencerPlatt / Staff / Getty Images; page 43: ©Frank and Helena / Getty Images; page 44: ©Heide Benser / Getty Images; page 45: ©7romawka7 / Getty Images

Library of Congress Cataloging-in-Publication Data

Library of Congress Cataloging-in-Publication Data has been filed and is available at catalog.loc.gov

Hardcover ISBN: 978-1-68450-783-2
Paperback ISBN: 978-1-68404-743-7

TABLE OF CONTENTS

CHAPTER 1

THE PROBLEM WITH POLLUTION

Sonja Michaluk grew up playing in ponds and streams in New Jersey. She loved water. She loved the creatures that lived there. Rocks hid toads and frogs. Snakes slithered along the water's edge. But her play spaces were under threat.

When Sonja was 11, she heard about a gas pipeline that might be built near her home. Pipelines carry gas or oil from one part of the country to another. Sometimes, pipelines leak and cause pollution. The liquid inside spills into the ground or runs into local water. It can even contaminate the air nearby.

Sonja began to gather **data** about local streams. She told people how the pipeline might harm the water. The pipeline was still built, but Sonja's research helped make sure it was done safely. By the time she was 17, Sonja had invented a way to check for water pollution. She could test the **organisms** that lived in the water.

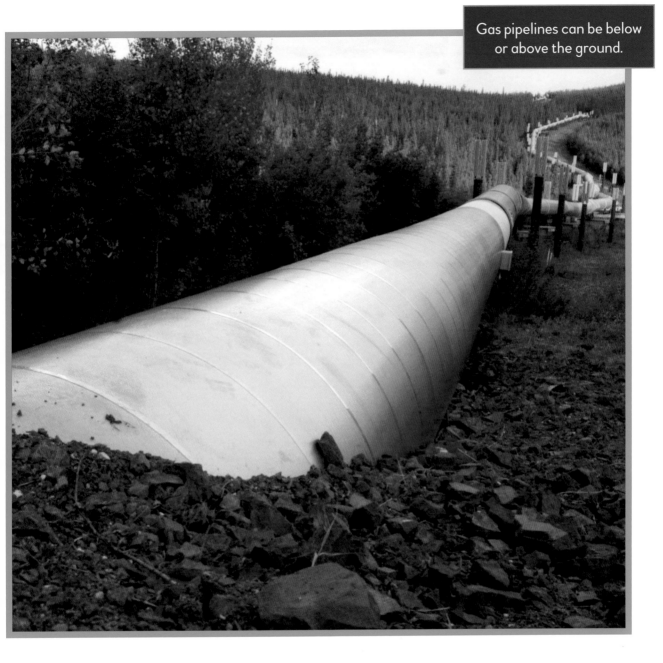

Gas pipelines can be below or above the ground.

Pollution is a big problem. It can make people and animals sick. Plants die. Harmful **greenhouse gases** are released. Some kinds of pollution are easy to spot. Others are nearly invisible. But all pollution causes big problems.

Smog in Los Angeles, California, looks like a layer of brown mist.

Pollution can be in the air or in the water. It can be liquid, solid, or gas. Air pollution is caused by harmful particles in the air. Forty percent of Americans live in areas with poor air quality. Soot and smog are two causes.

Soot is created when fuels are burned. Tiny, solid particles of chemicals, soil, dust, and other **allergens** stick around. Large amounts of soot can be seen on surfaces. Smog comes from smoke and fumes that are created by burning fuel. These **emissions** react with sunlight to create smog. Smog sometimes looks like dark clouds or brown fog in the sky. You can see it even on a sunny day.

Air pollution comes from many sources. A few are natural, like active volcanoes. But most air pollution is caused by humans. It comes from factories and power plants. Cars and trucks cause it too. Some home heating sources such as fireplaces and coal stoves can create pollution. Wildfires started by people pollute the air too.

How's Your Air?

You might have heard a weather report mention the AQI—that stands for Air Quality Index. Since 1968, the AQI has let people know how polluted the air is or might become in their area. Most countries have an AQI. The information changes from country to country depending on the pollutants in that country and its particular air quality standards. In the US, the AQI has six color-coded and numbered categories. It monitors the amounts of five pollutants in the air.

There are two main sources of pollution. Point source pollution comes from a single place. It might be a factory or a wastewater treatment plant. It could be an oil spill. It might also be a place where people dump garbage into the water. Nonpoint source pollution is usually caused by rainwater or wind. Particles are blown into waterways. Trash rolls into drains. Runoff from farms carries fertilizer and pesticides into rivers and oceans. Car exhaust and oil can make their way into the air and local water systems this way.

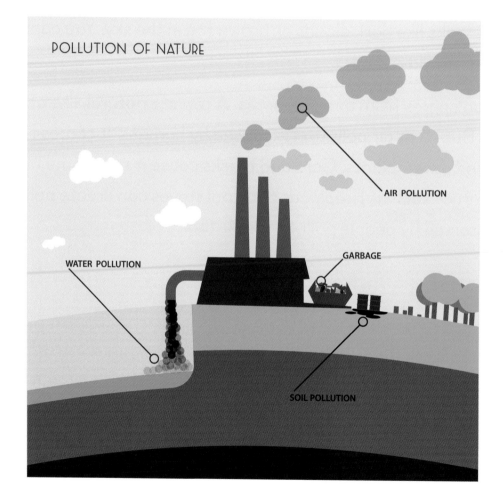

POLLUTION OF NATURE

AIR POLLUTION

WATER POLLUTION

GARBAGE

SOIL POLLUTION

Some factories dump waste directly into water. This is known as point source pollution.

Water pollution occurs when water mixes with chemicals or harmful bacteria. Water can dissolve almost anything. This means it gets dirty easily. Some polluted water looks unclean. It might be filled with garbage. It might be slimy. But some polluted water looks clean. That's because some pollutants are invisible. They don't even smell bad. This makes them extra dangerous.

Many of the same things pollute both the water and the air. Cars and factories are big causes of water and air pollution. Sometimes, toxic chemicals are washed into the water by rain. This is called runoff. Fertilizers and cleaning products are examples of pollutants that contaminate water. Human and animal waste runoff causes harmful bacteria to grow in water.

Polluted water is not safe to drink. Humans should not swim in it. It might cause sickness or rashes. It could even cause death. Anywhere between 884 million and 2.7 billion people around the world do not have fresh water to drink.

Blue-green algae looks like a thick layer of slime on the water's surface.

Lakes, streams, and rivers are known as fresh water sources. Around 70 percent of homes in the US get their water from these sources. But almost half of the country's rivers and streams are polluted. One-third of lakes in the US are not safe for swimming, fishing, or drinking.

Most of this pollution is caused by runoff. Fertilizer contains **nutrients** that help plants grow. But fertilizer also drains into the water. Too many nutrients cause many microorganisms to grow. Blue-green algae is one example. It is a type of bacteria. When too much of it grows in water, it is called **algal bloom**. This causes dead zones. These are areas where no fish or plants can live.

Mining and power plants can also contaminate fresh water. They pour chemicals and waste into the water. Rain sweeps **sewage**, pesticides, and oil into fresh water. And trash itself is just dirty. In some countries, rivers are filled with so much garbage that it affects waterways. This makes fishing difficult. Boats must travel around the trash. The trash also harms the creatures living in the water.

Where does your family's drinking water come from?

All water leads to the ocean. Polluted water travels just as fast as clean water does. The runoff from farms and factories flows to beautiful beaches. Algal blooms kill plants and smaller fish. Bigger fish starve. Predators die off. The blooms interrupt the ocean's life cycle.

Oil spills pollute huge sections of the ocean at once. Oil is found underground. Some oil seeps into the ocean naturally. But it can also be spilled from tankers that leak or wreck. Oil can also enter the ocean where oil is drilled, or through runoff.

Oil is very harmful to marine life. It spreads across the surface of the water. This is called a slick. The wind and waves spread the slick even more. Animals breathe or eat the oil. It sticks to their fur or feathers. It gets in their gills. It makes them sick. Sometimes, they get sick right away. But it can also affect their health over a long period of time.

The ocean isn't safe from trash pollution, either. Plastic is especially bad. Researchers think there is more plastic in the ocean than there are stars in the sky. Plastic never disappears. It just breaks down into smaller pieces as it floats through the waves. These bits are called microplastics. Fish think microplastics are food. They eat them, but they cannot digest them. Eventually, the fish starve to death. Larger pieces of plastic, like grocery bags, can trap or injure sea creatures. And plastic releases harmful chemicals into the water over time.

Around 8 million pieces of plastic end up in the ocean every day.

Families who live near factories cannot escape air pollution. For many, moving is not an option.

The harmful effects of pollution are more dangerous to people who are already sick. They might have an illness such as cancer, or a condition like asthma. Pollution is also more harmful to babies and elderly people.

People who live near factories suffer more from pollution. The homes near factories are usually in low-income neighborhoods. The people who live there are often **minorities** or are very poor. Latino, Asian, and Black Americans are exposed to as much as 34 percent more soot pollution than White Americans.

Soot can enter the bloodstream because it is made of tiny particles. It can cause severe breathing problems, heart disease, and even cancer. Dirty water can cause skin issues. It can also lead to stomach problems, ear and respiratory infections, and in some cases, death.

Air and water pollution are closely linked. Water absorbs pollution that is in the air. And millions breathe polluted air every day. Earth and its inhabitants suffer daily because of pollution. Scientists and world leaders work daily on ways to solve this problem.

Check out a weather app or watch your local weather report. Does the forecast mention air quality? How is the air quality in your area?

CHAPTER 2

CARING ABOUT WATER AND AIR

The **Industrial Revolution** was an exciting time in America. Cities grew. Factories began making new machines. Railroads let people and goods travel across the country. More people began moving to America looking for a better life.

Trains made life easier for Americans in the 1800s, but they also created more air pollution.

But more factories, more trains, and more people meant more pollution. City skies turned black with smog. People also created more waste. Cities weren't ready to handle it. Bays and rivers filled with garbage and sewage.

Over time, scientists started to see a connection between people's health and pollution. Both air and water pollution were getting out of control. Lawmakers realized it was time to make some rules about cleaning up.

The first Earth Day in 1970 included protests by college students across the US.

Why do you think laws had to be created to get people to take action against pollution?

In 1963, the US government passed the Clean Air Act. It was amended, or changed, in 1970 and 1990. Each change added a new set of laws about air pollution. The Clean Air Act made rules about the six most common air pollutants. They are carbon monoxide, nitrogen dioxide, **ozone**, sulfur dioxide, particulate matter, and lead. The Clean Air Act required the major sources of these pollutants to make changes. These included factories and vehicles.

Since 1970, air pollution has improved in America and in other places around the world. Cars now release fewer emissions. Factories and power plants put out fewer pollutants. As a result, there are smaller amounts of these six pollutants in the air. There is less **acid rain**, less smog, and fewer greenhouse gases in Earth's atmosphere. People also have fewer health problems caused by air pollution.

Part of the 1970 Clean Air Act was the founding of the Environmental Protection Agency (EPA). The EPA is a federal government organization. Its job is to make sure Americans have clean air, land, and water. Earth Day also began in 1970. Earth Day was proof that more than just scientists wanted to clean things up. American citizens wanted to help too.

Ohio's Cuyahoga River was polluted with oil and factory waste. Between 1868 and 1952, it caught fire nine times, causing $1.5 million in damage.

In 1969, an oil spill in California dumped millions of gallons of oil into the ocean. That same year, the Cuyahoga River caught fire. It was not the first time these things had happened. But now, Americans were more aware of the dangers of pollution.

The first Clean Water Act had been passed in 1948. It made rules about point sources of water pollution. It keeps rivers, streams, lakes, bays, oceans, and wetlands safe from industrial waste and intentional dumping. Factories and plants must get rid of waste safely. Dumping waste into water would not be allowed. In 1972, the act was amended, in part because of the Cuyahoga River fire. It would protect even more of the country's water.

Since 1972, the number of bodies of water in the US that are safe for swimming and fishing has doubled. Communities with water treatment plants also increased. Water treatment plants clean the water. Dirty water is treated until it is safe to drink. Before the Clean Water Act, only 8 million people were covered by water treatment plants. The law increased that number to 175 million.

Water treatment plants remove waste from water so it can be returned to the public water supply.

More people began to care about the environment in the 1970s. Industries wanted to reduce the damage they were doing. One was the energy industry. Energy is how we power homes, businesses, and vehicles. A common energy source is fossil fuel—coal, oil, and natural gas. These fuels can be burned or turned to liquid. But using them creates pollution. That's where clean, or green, energy comes in.

Green energy is a fuel source that is less harmful to the environment. Solar, wind, hydroelectricity, and biogas are a few common examples of green energy sources.

A large solar farm can create enough electricity to power more than 75,000 houses.

Clean Air Act Reduction in Pollution Since 1990

Carbon Monoxide ↓ 74%

Lead ↓ 82%

Nitrogen Dioxide ↓ 57%

Ozone ↓ 21%

Sulfur Dioxide ↓ 89%

Solar energy comes from the sun. Special panels are placed in sunny areas. Cells inside the panels turn sunlight into energy. Wind energy is collected by turbines. Wind causes blades on the turbines to turn like a fan. The turning blades spin a generator. That energy is turned into electricity. Solar panels can make electricity for a single home. But many wind turbines can create all the energy a community needs.

Hydroelectric energy is created by moving water. A generator is built near a river. The river's moving water pushes a turbine, which powers the generator. Hydroelectric energy is very powerful. It is also one of the most popular forms of green energy. There are around 2,400 hydroelectric power sources in the US.

Wind, sun, and water are great alternatives to fuels that cause pollution. They rely on energy sources that already exist in nature. But biomass is a green energy source that uses something humans make every day.

The Grand Coulee Dam in Washington State is the largest hydroelectric power source in the United States.

Biomass is any kind of plant or animal matter that can be used as fuel to create energy. Biomass pellets are made from forestry and agriculture by-products.

Biomass can mean trees or plants. Making a campfire is biomass energy. But biomass can also come from your local **landfill**. People throw away tons of food every year. When food waste rots, it makes a gas called methane. Too much methane can harm Earth's atmosphere. But methane can be used as biomass. Cows also make a lot of waste. But their manure can be used to create biomass energy too! The methane created by manure can be turned into biogas for powering vehicles and making electricity. Making energy from waste could solve two problems at once.

Garbage and cow manure are not the only materials that can be used to make natural gas. Corn, sugar, and vegetable oil can be used to make fuels called ethanol and biodiesel. These can be used to power vehicles. Although these fuels still have to be burned to create energy, they are not as bad for the environment. More cars that are newer can run on biofuels. Even huge 18-wheelers and big city buses are joining the biofuel industry.

Cars are a big cause of pollution. So carmakers are looking at other changes. One is low- or zero-emission vehicles. These cars and trucks do not release as much harmful exhaust, or smoke. Many of these vehicles have hybrid engines. This means they run on both fuel and electricity. Some vehicles are completely electric. Electric engines do not release any harmful emissions at all.

State laws are also reducing vehicle emissions. Many states require emissions inspections. This means a mechanic checks to make sure a vehicle's engine runs at acceptable levels. If more people chose clean energy sources to power their cars, homes, and businesses, pollution would continue to be less of a problem.

What are some things your city or community is doing to improve air quality? Can you rent a bike or scooter? Are public transportation vehicles hybrid?

Charging stations for electric cars are becoming more common.

Do You Have a Charger I Can Borrow?

If your phone's battery is low, it's pretty easy to find a place to charge it. But what happens when your electric car needs to be charged? Most electric vehicle (EV) owners can plug theirs into a standard outlet. They can also install a charging port that works faster. As EVs become more popular, more EV charging stations will show up in common public places, like the grocery store. They provide a quick charge and cost approximately the same as a tank of gas. Some places will even charge EVs for free. In 2021, there were around 46,000 EV charging stations in the US. That number grows as more people make the switch to fully electric vehicles.

CHAPTER 3

CLEANING UP

While the Clean Water Act and the Clean Air Act have helped reduce pollution in the US over the past 50 years, the problem hasn't gone away for good. Luckily, people are already thinking ahead. In 2021, the Climate Leadership and Environmental Action for our Nation's Future (CLEAN) Act was introduced. It called for many programs to reduce greenhouse gas emissions. It also added new rules for manufacturers and businesses. One of the main goals of the CLEAN Act is for there to be zero harmful greenhouse gases entering Earth's atmosphere by 2050.

Reducing Emissions One Car at a Time

Cars that run on fossil fuels are a major cause of harmful emissions. That's why these cars have their own built-in pollution fighter. Catalytic converters are small devices close to a car's exhaust pipe. Exhaust is the smoky air cars send out into the atmosphere as the engine burns fuel. It contains emissions that cause pollution. The catalytic converter cleans this exhaust before it leaves the car. These devices are made from a special material that acts as a catalyst, which is a substance that causes a chemical reaction. Catalytic converters burn the pollutants that come from the engine, making them less toxic as they enter the air outside the vehicle.

Since 1975, all cars in the United States have been required to have catalytic converters.

A great deal of air pollution comes from factories. Current and future laws can help manufacturers change the way they operate. Using clean energy to run machines will keep many common pollutants out of the air.

But not every factory can quickly or easily switch its energy source. New technology can help cut pollution for these factories. Special devices called oxidizers destroy pollutants with high temperatures before they enter the air. Wet scrubbers are another way to clean the air. They trap pollution in liquid droplets. Oxidizers and scrubbers can keep up to 99 percent of pollutants out of the atmosphere.

Many cities around the world are using technology to keep their air clean too. Three scientists invented a special paint called Airlite. It has become very popular in Mexico City. This paint contains a special substance. It uses light to turn toxic pollutants into salt particles. The salt turns into a protective layer for buildings. It keeps solar heat from being absorbed, so energy costs are lowered. Every square foot of Airlite sprayed does the same work to purify the air as a forest of the same size.

In addition to reducing pollutants in the air, Airlite paint also eliminates bad odors and repels dust and dirt.

Green City Solutions is using moss and other tiny plants to create green roofs over bus stops and other public areas in London, England.

In London, England, a company called Arborea is testing their BioSolar Leaf. The panel contains thousands of tiny plants such as moss and **phytoplankton**. A panel with the surface area of one tree can clean the air as well as 100 trees can. Green City Solutions is another company introduced in London. Their CityTrees are air filters made of moss. The structures clean the air and provide shade in high-population areas.

And in the US, a company called 3M is making more than office supplies. They sell roofing products for homes made of smog-eating particles. When the particles are heated by the sun, they turn air pollution into water-soluble ions. These and other inventions, along with changes in manufacturing, are working together to lower air pollution around the world.

But ordinary people can help too. Families who use less energy lower their pollution contribution. Cutting back on energy use means power plants don't have to work as hard. Time off for power plants means less pollution too. Turning off lights, using low-energy light bulbs, and unplugging electronics when they are not being used are easy ways to cut back on energy use. Using energy-saving appliances helps too.

Some families drive hybrid cars. Some take public transportation, walk, or bike. All of these are better for the environment. But not all families have an energy-saving car. Not everyone lives by a bus stop. Driving less by limiting errands to one day each week can still help. Making sure the family car is in good shape is also important. Regular oil changes and tire checks keep a car running properly. A tuned-up car doesn't cause as much pollution.

Families can also avoid products that contain volatile organic compounds (VOCs). VOCs are in many cleaning products. They are also found in paints, glues, and pesticides. VOCs are a major source of indoor air pollution. Individuals are advised to use a natural cleaner instead. Many companies are now making low- or no-VOC products too. Read the labels before you use them. *Non-toxic, plant-based*, and *biodegradable* are all words to look for.

Families who choose to walk or bike can help keep harmful pollution out of Earth's atmosphere.

Using pavers instead of concrete helps reduce the amount of runoff from fertilizer, pesticides, and cleaning products.

Saying no to VOC products helps reduce water pollution as well. VOCs used in homes can easily enter the water supply. Heavily paved areas like sidewalks and driveways are easy paths for these chemicals. From there, rainwater picks them up and carries them into the water supply. Washing cars on grass or rocks helps keep this from happening. Instead of washing away, chemicals are absorbed into the soil. Soil is a natural filter. Water slips through, but the bad stuff is left behind.

Compost is another natural filter. When food scraps and yard waste are left to rot in landfills, they make too many greenhouse gases. But composting them reduces greenhouse gases. It also makes a natural fertilizer. Composting can help reduce both air and water pollution by keeping natural waste out of landfills.

Picking up other kinds of waste can reduce water pollution. Keeping sidewalks and local parks free of litter keeps trash from getting washed into streams and rivers. Using less creates less waste. Reusable water bottles and straws keep plastic versions from filling up rivers and oceans.

Composting food and yard waste creates a natural fertilizer called humus.

Plastic containers that are dirty can't be recycled. Does your family wash bottles and other containers before they go in the recycling bin?

Ocean Cleanup removed around 500,000 pounds (235,505 kg) of plastic from the ocean in 2020. But the real solution is to stop using single-use plastic.

Keeping trash out of the ocean is important. But there is a lot of trash there already. What do we do about that? A company called Ocean Cleanup is trying to help. Ocean Cleanup is one of several groups that is using technology to solve the water pollution problem. The company's devices work with the ocean's natural current. Their huge U-shaped barriers collect trash in hanging nets. Oceans aren't the only place their barriers work. They can also collect trash from rivers. There are currently three ocean-cleaning devices and three river-cleaning devices in operation. Ocean Cleanup is also exploring ways to create greener cleaning devices. Minimizing the effect on ocean animals and preventing further pollution is part of their future goal.

Kando is another company concerned with clean water. While Ocean Cleanup is removing trash that is in the water, Kando targets chemical pollution. Their Pulse system keeps track of areas of point-source pollution. The water is always being watched. The system alerts officials when the water is too dirty. This makes it possible to stop the pollution from going further or getting larger. Pulse can also locate the cause. Stopping it at its source is the most effective way to get rid of it.

Water is a limited resource, and clean water is rare in some places. It is more important than ever to use it wisely. What is one way you can save water in your home?

About 100,000 rivers and streams, including 150 major rivers, empty into the Chesapeake Bay.

Armed with data, groups in the US are cleaning up three important bodies of water: the Great Lakes, the Chesapeake Bay, and the Florida Everglades. The Great Lakes have been polluted by farm runoff, trash, and factory waste. These lakes provide drinking water to more than 30 million people. The Great Lakes contain one-fifth of the entire world's fresh surface water. The lakes are also home to hundreds of fish species and thousands of birds and other animals. The land around them is excellent for farming.

The Chesapeake Bay is another important US body of water. It is also one of the dirtiest. The Chesapeake Bay is located in Virginia and Maryland. It is the largest estuary in the country. This means it contains salt water and fresh water. Several major rivers empty into the bay. Then, that water flows into the ocean. Many people and animals need the waters of the Chesapeake Bay.

Many need the Florida Everglades too. These wetlands are a series of connected waters. They provide drinking water to many Florida residents. Many unique plant and animal species live there. Healthy trees and plants clean the air through **photosynthesis**. They release oxygen back into the atmosphere. Without clean water, green things won't grow. But the Everglades have been polluted by farm runoff. Local and national cleanup efforts are in place to restore these important bodies of water.

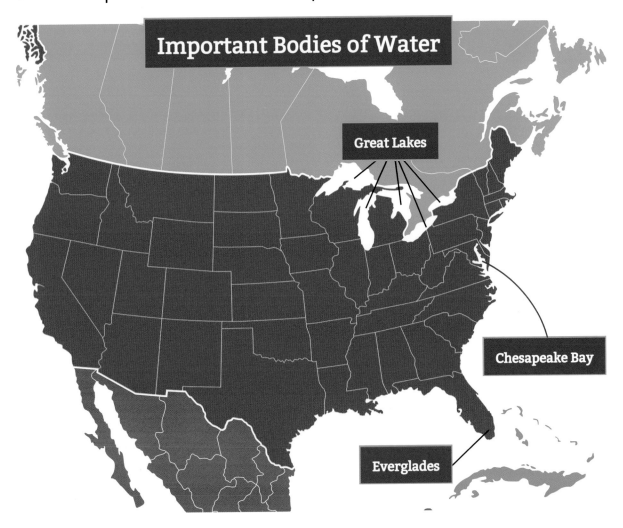

Important Bodies of Water

Great Lakes

Chesapeake Bay

Everglades

Pollution is not just an American problem. Bad air still causes 7 million deaths around the world each year. At least two billion people in the world do not have access to clean water. In countries where there are no rules about pollution, water goes untreated. Factories fill the air with smog. The United States is part of global efforts to change this.

Factories create around one-quarter of Earth's greenhouse gases.

The United Nations Climate Change Conference was first held in 1995. It takes place every year. Leaders from many countries meet. They work together to solve world environmental issues. Pollution is the cause of many of those issues.

In 2015, the Paris Agreement was written. Each country that signed the agreement promised to reduce emissions of pollutants. This means creating new laws and making changes in the way people work, drive, and live.

Leaders from all over the world gather each year to create solutions for the climate crisis.

One of the greatest impacts of the Clean Air and Clean Water Acts was community awareness. The early 1970s was the beginning of the **environmental movement**. More people started caring about the world around them. Starting the EPA and Earth Day have helped. Both our air and water are cleaner than ever.

But there is still a lot of work to do. Laws can only do so much to change people's habits. Bigger changes can occur when people work together. Truly stopping air and water pollution will require every citizen of the world to do their part.

On September 26, 2020, people participating in International Coastal Cleanup Day removed 5.2 million pounds (2.4 million kg) of plastic from beaches around the world.

Activity 1:

Create a family pollution prevention plan—come up with ways within your family unit that can help you reduce pollution.

MATERIALS:

- paper
- pens/pencils

PROCEDURE:

- Have a family meeting and talk about how you can work together to reduce pollution and waste less water.

- Make a list of around five to seven actions you can take. These could include turning off lights, turning off the water while brushing your teeth, creating a compost bin, or switching to natural cleaners.

- Once you have agreed on your list, write down your action plan. Make a copy for each room in the house and post it in a place where everyone can see it.

Activity 2:

As a class, create a poster campaign to educate your school community about how to reduce water and air pollution.

MATERIALS:

- markers
- poster board

PROCEDURE:

- Make a list of problems contributing to air and water pollution, and then come up with a strategy or two for each one that you and your classmates can do. Use this book to help you. Do further research online or in your school library.

- Create colorful posters that teach others about how they can help solve the pollution problem.

- Hang the posters around your school in places where they can be seen easily.

GLOSSARY

ACID RAIN (AS-uhd RAYN): rainfall made acidic by the addition of sulfur and nitrogen oxides from burned fossil fuels

ALGAL BLOOM (AL-juhl BLOOM): overgrowth of microorganisms in water that causes a colored scum on the water's surface

ALLERGENS (ALL-ur-jehnz): substances that cause an extreme response in the body's immune system

COMPOST (COM-post): to mix food and yard waste together with soil to create a natural fertilizer called humus

DATA (DAY-tuh): information

EMISSIONS (uh-MISH-uhns): substances released into the air

ENVIRONMENTAL MOVEMENT (en-VY-ruhn-MEN-tuhl MOVE-ment): a worldwide effort involving multiple people, activist groups, and government organizations to address issues related to nature and the health of the planet

GREENHOUSE GASES (GREEN-hows GAS): substances in Earth's atmosphere that trap heat energy from the sun

INDUSTRIAL REVOLUTION (in-DUS-tree-uhl rev-uh-LOO-shuhn): a period from 1790 to 1860 when work began to be done by machines, rather than by hand

LANDFILL (LAND-fill): a place where garbage is buried

MINORITIES (my-NOR-uh-tees): groups that make up less than half of a large group

NUTRIENTS (NOO-tree-yunts): chemical compounds used by living things to function properly

ORGANISMS (OR-guh-niz-uhms): living things

OZONE (OH-zone): a form of oxygen that creates a layer high above Earth and protects the planet from the Sun's harmful rays

PHOTOSYNTHESIS (foh-toh-SIN-thuh-sis): a process plants use to make food and oxygen

PHYTOPLANKTON (FY-toh-playnk-tuhn): microscopic plants

SEWAGE (SEW-uhj): waste matter carried away from homes and businesses in drains

FOR MORE INFORMATION

BOOKS

Bell, Lucy. *You Can Change the World: The Kids' Guide to a Better Planet.* Kansas City, MO: McMeel Publishing, 2020.

Furgang, Kathy. *Clean Water For All.* New York, NY: Power Kids Press, 2020.

Rossiter, Brienna. *Saving Earth's Air.* Lake Elmo, MN: Focus Readers, 2022.

WEBSITES

Air Pollution

https://www.ducksters.com/science/environment/air_pollution.php
Learn about air pollution, what causes it, and what you can do to help.

It's Bad for the Environment (and People Too!)

https://kids.niehs.nih.gov/topics/pollution/index.htm
Breaks down pollution and answers your important questions.

Pollution

https://kids.nationalgeographic.com/science/article/pollution
Find out how pollution affects Earth and the creatures who live on it.

Water Pollution

https://www.ducksters.com/science/environment/water_pollution.php
Facts about water pollution, including ways to help clean it up.

INDEX

ABOUT THE AUTHOR

Heather DiLorenzo Williams is a writer and educator with a passion for seeing readers of all ages connect with others through stories and personal experiences. She enjoys running, reading, and watching sports. Heather lives in North Carolina with her husband and two children.